PRODUCTIVITY
FOR
AUTHORS

A Companion
Workbook

FIND TIME TO WRITE, ORGANIZE YOUR AUTHOR
LIFE, AND DECIDE WHAT REALLY MATTERS

Joanna Penn

Published by Curl Up Press

Requests to publish work from this book should be sent to:
joanna@CurlUpPress.com

Cover and Interior Design: JD Smith

Printed by Amazon KDP Print

www.CurlUpPress.com

Contents

Introduction

"If you don't produce, you won't thrive no matter
how skilled or talented you are."

Cal Newport, *Deep Work*

If you have more time to write and you use that time effectively, you will become a better writer and you will produce more books. Creativity is at the heart of what we do, but productivity is the only way to get your words out into the world.

Finished products — print books, ebooks, audiobooks — only happen when you finish your writing project. So, **you need to be productive in order to be a successful writer**.

Of course, you need to fit writing around the rest of your life, so optimizing the time you have is critical. But optimizing is not about short-term hacks. It's about sustainable productivity and doing the best you can with what you have in order to achieve more. The real question is: What do *you* want to achieve?

I've been writing and publishing for over a decade and for many of those years, I focused on 'doing.' I love making lists and ticking items off as evidence of achievement, and I am very good at getting a lot done. But a few years back, I realized that I was spending my time doing a whole load of things that weren't helping me to reach my goals. I was often busy for the sake of being busy.

I took a step back to evaluate how I was spending my time and why. I read lots of books on productivity and used many of the ideas to reboot my writing and creative business. These days, I'm much more productive in terms of what I create, but also have more time for my health and lifestyle goals.

In *Productivity for Authors*, I shared my lessons learned in order to help you become more productive and, hopefully, save you time, money and heartache along the way. In this Workbook edition, I hope you can take those lessons and apply them to your own author journey.

> "Productivity is the amount of useful output created for every hour of work we do. Did I spend my day producing enough benefit for all the time invested?"
>
> *Seth Godin, Business/busyness*

* * *

Note: There are affiliate links within this workbook to products and services that I recommend and use personally. This means that I receive a small percentage of sales with no extra cost to you, and in some cases, you may receive a discount for using my links. I only recommend products and services that I believe are great for authors, so I hope you find them useful.

1. What is stopping you from being productive?

Before we get started, it's important to take a step back and look at the bigger picture. No magic tool or technique is going to fix your productivity unless you also consider your mindset and the obstacles that are in your way. Be honest with yourself. There's no one here to judge you.

What is stopping you from being productive in your writing life?

_____

_____

_____

_____

_____

_____

_____

_____

_____

What is your why? What drives you to write? Why do you want to be more productive? What will keep you going when things get tough?

_____

_____

_____

_____

_____

_____

_____

_____

_____

_____

_____

_____

_____

_____

_____

_____

Who are you? What is your self-definition? When you say "I am a writer," is it reflected in how you live your life?

"Who you are, what you think, feel and do, what you love is the sum of what you focus on."

Cal Newport, *Deep Work*

* * *

Further Notes and Ideas:

2. Goal setting

"If you work on too many ideas at once, you run the great risk of all your ideas constantly being half finished."

Donald Roos, *Don't Read this Book:*
Time Management for Creative People

What are your goals?

_____

_____

_____

_____

_____

_____

_____

_____

_____

_____

Which one primary goal will you focus on?

_____

_____

_____

_____

_____

_____

_____

_____

_____

_____

_____

_____

_____

_____

_____

_____

_____

_____

_____

What stage of the author journey are you on? What is the best goal for your current stage? What can wait until later?

_____

_____

_____

_____

_____

_____

_____

_____

_____

_____

_____

_____

_____

_____

_____

_____

_____

_____

Further Notes and Ideas:

3. Deadlines

How much time do you need for your book?
(or at least for the first draft?)

_____

_____

_____

_____

_____

_____

_____

_____

_____

_____

_____

Get out your calendar, count the months and put in your deadline date. Have you completed this?

_____

_____

_____

_____

_____

_____

_____

_____

_____

_____

_____

_____

_____

_____

_____

_____

What can you do to make yourself more accountable?

_____

_____

_____

_____

_____

_____

_____

_____

_____

_____

_____

_____

_____

_____

_____

Further Notes and Ideas:

4. Busy work vs. important work

"The biggest waste of time is to do well something
that we need not do at all."

Gretchen Rubin, *Better Than Before*

Write down everything you have to do, or review
your list. How much of it is 'busy work'? How much
can wait until a later stage of the process?

_____

_____

_____

_____

_____

_____

_____

_____

_____

_____

How are you balancing busy work with important work and urgent work? What things fall into these categories for you?

_____

_____

_____

_____

_____

_____

_____

_____

_____

_____

_____

_____

_____

_____

"Busy is not your job. Busy doesn't get you what you seek. Busy isn't the point. Value creation is."

Seth Godin

Further Notes and Ideas:

5. Saying no and setting boundaries

"The single most important change you can make in your working habits is to switch to creative work first, reactive work second."

Jocelyn K. Glei, *Manage Your-Day-To-Day*

What are you struggling to say no to? Where do you need to set boundaries to protect your creative time? (even if it's for a limited timeframe)

_____

_____

_____

_____

_____

_____

_____

_____

_____

_____

Write your own Not To Do list

_____

_____

_____

_____

_____

_____

_____

_____

_____

_____

_____

_____

_____

_____

_____

_____

_____

How much are you giving into distraction?
Have you turned off notifications on your phone
and computer?

_____

_____

_____

_____

_____

_____

_____

_____

_____

_____

_____

_____

_____

_____

_____

_____

What could you do if you are still struggling?

_____

_____

_____

_____

_____

_____

_____

_____

_____

_____

_____

_____

_____

_____

_____

_____

_____

Further Notes and Ideas:

6. How to find the time to write

"Write at the edges of the day."

Toni Morrison

Are you scheduling your writing time at the moment? If not, why not? Where is your resistance?

_____

_____

_____

_____

_____

_____

_____

_____

_____

_____

Do you have an accurate view of how you spend your time? If not, track a week of activities including TV and gaming.

_____

_____

_____

_____

_____

_____

_____

_____

_____

_____

_____

_____

_____

_____

_____

_____

How much do you really want this? What are you going to give up in order to find time for your writing?

_____

_____

_____

_____

_____

_____

_____

_____

_____

_____

_____

_____

_____

_____

_____

Have you done the calculation on how much time you need for that first draft? Or revision time or whatever you need.

_____

_____

_____

_____

_____

_____

_____

_____

_____

_____

_____

_____

_____

_____

_____

_____

Have you scheduled your next block of writing time?
How are you going to make sure you turn up?

_____

_____

_____

_____

_____

_____

_____

_____

_____

_____

_____

_____

_____

_____

"On the field of the Self, stand a knight and a dragon. You are the
knight, resistance is the dragon. The battle must be fought every day."

Steven Pressfield, *The War of Art*

Further Notes and Ideas:

7. Make the most of
your writing time

"Habit tracking keeps your eye on the ball. You're focused on the process rather than the results. It's remarkable what you can build if you just don't stop."

James Clear, *Atomic Habits*

What does your creative location and setup look like? How can you make this your routine?

_____

_____

_____

_____

_____

_____

_____

_____

_____

_____

How will you stop distractions, interruptions and procrastination?

_____

_____

_____

_____

_____

_____

_____

_____

_____

_____

_____

_____

_____

_____

_____

_____

_____

Have you tried timed writing? How did it work out
for you? If not, why not?

_____

_____

_____

_____

_____

_____

_____

_____

_____

_____

_____

_____

_____

_____

_____

How will you measure your progress?

How could you write faster?

_____

_____

_____

_____

_____

_____

_____

_____

_____

_____

_____

_____

_____

_____

_____

_____

_____

_____

Are there any other ways that will help you make the most of your time writing?

"Don't wait for the muse ... he's a hardheaded guy who's
not susceptible to a lot of creative fluttering. This isn't the Ouija
board or the spirit-world we're talking about here, but just another
job like laying pipe or driving long-haul trucks."

Stephen King, *On Writing*

Further Notes and Ideas:

8. Dictation

Why might you consider dictation? How might it help your writing?

_____

_____

_____

_____

_____

_____

_____

_____

_____

_____

_____

_____

What's stopping you from dictating? How can you work through those issues in order to try it?

_____

_____

_____

_____

_____

_____

_____

_____

_____

_____

_____

_____

_____

_____

_____

_____

What method of dictation might work for you?

What tools do you need to get started?

_____

_____

_____

_____

_____

_____

_____

_____

_____

_____

_____

_____

_____

_____

_____

"**Embrace dictation as a productivity tool.** It's a weapon in your writing arsenal and your workflow. **In the next 10 years, if you're not embracing voice, you will be behind in the same way as if you don't have a smartphone right now.** You're missing out on a lot of technological help."

Scott Baker, _The Writer's Guide to Training your Dragon_

Further Notes and Ideas:

_____

_____

_____

_____

_____

_____

_____

_____

_____

_____

_____

_____

_____

_____

_____

_____

_____

_____

9. Co-writing and collaboration

Why do you want to co-write or collaborate with another writer?

_____

_____

_____

_____

_____

_____

_____

_____

_____

_____

_____

What are the possible pros and cons?

_____

_____

_____

_____

_____

_____

_____

_____

_____

_____

_____

_____

_____

_____

_____

_____

_____

_____

_____

_____

Why are you and your proposed co-writer a good fit as a partnership? (or as a group)

_____

_____

_____

_____

_____

_____

_____

_____

_____

_____

_____

_____

_____

_____

_____

_____

What are some of the aspects you need to discuss upfront?

_____

_____

_____

_____

_____

_____

_____

_____

_____

_____

_____

_____

_____

_____

_____

_____

_____

_____

How will you practically work together?

Have you laid out your working process, deadlines, money, etc., in a written document and agreed it?

How will you make sure that your collaboration works for the long term?

Further Notes and Ideas:

10. Outsourcing

Why are you considering outsourcing? If not now,
then when might you need it?

_____

_____

_____

_____

_____

_____

_____

_____

_____

_____

_____

Do you currently work with different freelancers?
How much do you do yourself? How much do you
WANT to do yourself?

_____

_____

_____

_____

_____

_____

_____

_____

_____

_____

_____

_____

_____

_____

_____

_____

What are your zones of incompetence, competence, excellence and genius?

Incompetence

_____

_____

_____

_____

Competence

_____

_____

_____

_____

Excellence

_____

_____

_____

_____

Genius

_____

_____

_____

Sometimes you have to give up areas of
Competence and Excellence in order to make time
for your Zone of Genius.

Are you spending too much time in the
wrong zone?

_____

_____

_____

_____

_____

What is stopping you from hiring more help right
now? How can you remedy that so you have more
time to create?

_____

_____

_____

_____

_____

_____

_____

_____

Make a list of everything you do, and split it into logical groupings

---

Eliminate tasks that really don't need doing – or don't need doing right now. Could any of the tasks be automated?

Where can you look for freelancers or virtual assistants?

_____

_____

_____

_____

_____

_____

How will you work effectively with them?

_____

_____

_____

_____

_____

_____

_____

"It's better to disappoint a few people over small things than to surrender your dreams for an empty inbox."

Jocelyn K. Glei, *Manage Your Day-To-Day*

Further Notes and Ideas:

11. Productivity tools

Are there parts of your writing and author business processes that could be improved with a tool?

_____

_____

_____

_____

_____

_____

_____

_____

_____

_____

_____

_____

_____

Which tool/s could help you to become more productive?

_____

_____

_____

_____

_____

_____

_____

_____

_____

_____

_____

_____

_____

_____

_____

_____

_____

_____

_____

Further Notes and Ideas:

12. The productive writer mindset

This is just an overview on mindset as it relates to productivity. For more detail, check out *The Successful Author Mindset*, also available as a Workbook edition.

What is stopping you from being productive? Go deeper into each answer. For example, if you said writer's block, then dig to the next level and work out what that block might really be.

_____

_____

_____

_____

_____

_____

_____

_____

_____

_____

Who do you compare yourself to and why? Is there a way to use that as an inspiration for your next steps?

_____

_____

_____

_____

_____

_____

_____

_____

_____

_____

_____

_____

_____

_____

_____

_____

How will you overcome these mindset issues to be more productive?

_____

_____

_____

_____

_____

_____

_____

_____

_____

_____

_____

_____

_____

"We won't make ourselves more creative and productive by copying other people's habits, even the habits of geniuses. We must know our own nature and what habits serve us best."

Gretchen Rubin, _Better Than Before_

Further Notes and Ideas:

13. Healthy productivity

This is just an overview of how health can impact productivity. For more detail, check out *The Healthy Writer: Reduce your Pain, Improve your Health and Build a Writing Career for the Long Term*, by Joanna Penn and Dr. Euan Lawson.

> Disclaimer: I am not a medical doctor and this chapter is based on my opinion and experience. I'm also not going to be talking in detail about mental health. Please seek medical advice from your doctor if you have health issues.

* * *

Why are your physical and mental health important for productivity?

Think of your health like an onion. What is the first layer you need to tackle? What's bothering you right now?

_____

_____

_____

_____

_____

_____

_____

_____

_____

_____

_____

_____

_____

_____

_____

_____

_____

_____

Where is your resistance around health issues? (Food and movement are common ones!)

How is your sleep? How can you improve it?

_____

_____

_____

_____

_____

_____

_____

_____

_____

_____

_____

_____

_____

_____

_____

_____

_____

_____

How else are you going to ensure self-care in order to be productive for the long term?

_____

_____

_____

_____

_____

_____

_____

What can you do in the next 24 hours that will start you in the right direction?

_____

_____

_____

_____

_____

_____

_____

_____

Further Notes and Ideas:

Further Notes and Ideas:

Further Notes and Ideas:

Further Notes and Ideas:

Further Notes and Ideas:

Further Notes and Ideas:

Further Notes and Ideas:

Further Notes and Ideas:

Further Notes and Ideas:

Further Notes and Ideas:

Further Notes and Ideas:

Further Notes and Ideas:

Further Notes and Ideas:

Further Notes and Ideas:

Further Notes and Ideas:

Conclusion and next steps

There are a lot of tips and tools in this book and I hope that you have discovered some new ideas that will help you to become more productive. But I don't want to leave you overwhelmed, so here are my top three tips, the things that should provide you with the most leverage for your next steps. If you do nothing else, do these.

(1) Choose your focus and eliminate everything else

So much of what we do isn't necessary in order to achieve our goals. If you can pare back all those extra activities, even for a short time, you will have the time and headspace to beat overwhelm and achieve your writing goals.

(2) Schedule your creative time and don't miss it

If you want to write your first book, produce more books, or make more money with your writing, then you must do this. No excuses. Start using a schedule and make your creative time sacred.

(3) Sort out your sleep

Physical health is critical to productivity as well as happiness, and sleep is the best way to recover from a busy day, recharge for tomorrow and give your creative mind time to figure out interesting things for you to write next.

* * *

Now it's time for you to put this book into action and become more productive while I get back to writing the next book!

Appendix 1: Bibliography

You can find a downloadable version of this at:

TheCreativePenn.com/productivitydownload

Atomic Habits: An Easy and Proven Way to Build Good Habits and Break Bad Ones — James Clear

Better Than Before: What I Learned About Making and Breaking Habits — To Sleep More, Quit Sugar, Procrastinate Less and Generally Build a Happier Life — Gretchen Rubin

Co-writing a Book: Collaboration and Co-creation for Writers — Joanna Penn and J. Thorn

Daily Rituals: How Artists Work — Mason Currey

Deep Work: Rules for Focused Success in a Distracted World — Cal Newport

Dictate Your Book: How to Write your Book Faster, Better and Smarter — Monica Leonelle

Don't Read this Book: Time Management for Creative People — Donald Roos

Essentialism: The Disciplined Pursuit of Less — Greg McKeown

Foolproof Dictation: A Non-Nonsense System for Effective and Rewarding Dictation — Christopher Downing

How to Make a Living with your Writing — Joanna Penn

How to Write Non-Fiction: Turn Your Knowledge into Words — Joanna Penn

Manage Your Day-To-Day edited — Jocelyn K. Glei (editor)

On Being a Dictator: Using Dictation to be a Better Writer — Kevin J. Anderson

On Writing: A Memoir of the Craft — Stephen King

Productivity for Creative People: How to Get Creative Work Done in an Always On World — Mark McGuinness

Seth Godin blog post on busyness - https://seths.blog/2018/07/busyness/

Steal Like An Artist: 10 Things Nobody Told You About Being Creative — Austin Kleon

The Artist's Way — Julia Cameron

The Big Leap — Gay Hendricks

The Compound Effect: Jumpstart Your Income, Your Life, Your Success — Darren Hardy

The Healthy Writer: Reduce your Pain, Improve your Health, and Build a Writing Career for the Long Term — Joanna Penn and Dr. Euan Lawson

The ONE Thing: The Surprisingly Simple Truth Behind Extraordinary Results — Gary Keller and Jay Papasan

The War of Art: Break Through the Blocks and Win Your Inner Creative Battles — Steven Pressfield

The Writers Guide to Training your Dragon: Mastering Speech Recognition Software to Dictate your Book and Supercharge your Writing Workflow — Scott Baker

Turning Pro: Tap Your Inner Power and Create Your Life's Work — Steven Pressfield

Virtual Freedom: How to Work with Virtual Staff to Buy More Time, Become More Productive, and Build Your Dream Business — Chris Ducker

Why We Sleep: Unlocking the Power of Sleep and Dreams — Matthew Walker

* * *

You can find all my books for authors at:

www.TheCreativePenn.com/books

Most of them are available in audiobook format, as well as ebook and paperback.

About Joanna Penn

Joanna Penn, writing as J.F.Penn, is an Award-nominated, New York Times and USA Today bestselling author of thrillers and dark fantasy, as well as writing inspirational non-fiction for authors.

She is an international professional speaker, podcaster, and award-winning entrepreneur. She lives in Bath, England with her husband and enjoys a nice G&T.

Joanna's award-winning site for writers www.TheCreativePenn.com helps people to write, publish and market their books through articles, audio, video and online products as well as live workshops.

Love thrillers? www.JFPenn.com

Love travel? www.BooksAndTravel.page

Connect with Joanna
www.TheCreativePenn.com
joanna@TheCreativePenn.com

www.twitter.com/thecreativepenn
www.facebook.com/TheCreativePenn
www.Instagram.com/jfpennauthor
www.youtube.com/thecreativepenn

More Books And Courses From Joanna Penn

Non-Fiction Books for Authors

How to Write Non-Fiction

How to Market a Book

How to Make a Living with your Writing

Productivity for Authors

Business for Authors

The Healthy Writer

Successful Self-Publishing

Co-writing a Book

Public Speaking for Authors,
Creatives and Other Introverts

Career Change

www.TheCreativePenn.com/books

Courses for authors

How to Write a Novel: From Idea to First Draft to Finished Manuscript

How to Write Non-Fiction:
Turn your Knowledge into Words

Productivity for Authors

Content Marketing for Fiction Authors

www.TheCreativePenn.com/courses

Thriller novels as J.F.Penn

The ARKANE supernatural thriller series:

Stone of Fire #1
Crypt of Bone #2
Ark of Blood #3
One Day In Budapest #4
Day of the Vikings #5
Gates of Hell #6
One Day in New York #7
Destroyer of Worlds #8
End of Days #9
Valley of Dry Bones #10

If you like **crime thrillers with an edge of the supernatural**, join Detective Jamie Brooke and museum researcher Blake Daniel, in the London Crime Thriller trilogy:

Desecration #1
Delirium #2
Deviance #3

The Mapwalker dark fantasy series

Map of Shadows #1
Map of Plagues #2

Risen Gods

American Demon Hunters: Sacrifice

A Thousand Fiendish Angels:
Short stories based on Dante's Inferno

The Dark Queen:
An Underwater Archaeology Short Story

More books coming soon.

You can sign up to be notified of new releases, giveaways and pre-release specials - plus, get a free book!

www.JFPenn.com/free

Made in the USA
Monee, IL
06 December 2019

18062904R00056